MW00698926

Also by Dillon Haas

Swirling Shadows

OF BLOOD AND INK

DILLON HAAS

All rights reserved. Printed in the United States of America. No part of this book may be used or reproduced in any manner whatsoever without written permission, except in the case of brief quotations embodied in critical articles or reviews.

Of Blood and Ink

Copyright © 2020 Dillon Haas

Book and Cover Design by Dillon Haas

ISBN: 978-1-09832-610-4

CONTENTS

| LOVE |

Good Morning

You hear the closing click of her iPhone,
before you feel the warmth of her body as she snuggles you.

Your eyes squint at the clock – you've slept in.

But the kisses she paints with her tongue on your neck,
and the goosebumps that race down your skin,
let you know she's not mad.

She awoke an hour ago – reading and surfing through memes as if
smiling at cartoons of the daily newspaper,
but generations have changed and so have you.

Tossing over, your fingers trace her curves, before
teasing through her hair.

She loves it – her eyes rolling back, and a smile that refuses to
leave her face.

A few seconds of comfortable silence goes by, before she asks if
you'd like some coffee.

You smile, kiss her on her forehead, and nod.

Sometimes you have to remind yourself she's real.

Moon of My Life

In the moments of getting lost in laughter together
at the edge of my bed,

I find myself sitting curbside within my head –
reciting and reminiscing the day Fate wove you
into my life with a sparing thread.

Strong and silent,
you've helped me find my voice in
becoming a giant amongst men;

not just with the paper and pen but,
so too, within the world we live in.

You call me your Viking, and I – my Goddess

But loving you is something, in which, even I
don't possess the words to paint you in.

Takeout for Two

Rain gently taps her song upon your window,
your windshield wipers making the beat for her.

It's that time of the month –
but you're already on your way home from
copping some snackies.

Just another five minutes,
until you're home and get to make her happy.

Cheesecake and salads –
tonight's wholesome remedy.

Clothes soaked,
water dripping from your nose,
bags in hand,
you open the door.

Though, little does she know,
that look she gives you of "you're the best," is a look
even the Greeks would have went to war for.

Caffeine Drip

I can't get enough of you,
keep sipping and feeling the rush of you –
though the heart palpitations
warn me I have to discontinue,
I continue,
until
the scare becomes real
and my chest tightens.

But,
I'd rather risk it
than risk losing that feeling of having you.

Words Unspoken

I love those moments when

something happens in public and

your eyes smile to mine. Words lose their voice,

for that one look shares a whole conversation.

Dillon Haas

Dime Piece

One look at you and
my body feels your presence –

beauty that makes even a blind man look twice.

But if I stare for too long,
I could end up as he;

burned by the sun.

In a Sea Of

In a sea of endless stories to faces that don't add to your own,
I'd never thought I'd come across yours.

*

Sand is pouring over me,
blackness clouding my vision,
my lungs.

My last breath is taken away
as easily as the day you told me you loved me;

a moment in time, forever encapsulated –
ironic, as my hand sifts amongst the grains that buried me.

I fell in love with you, the very first few conversations we had –
the way your unforgiving eyes smiled as they
undressed and analyzed me.

So, I waited.
I waited, because I knew,
you too would feel what I felt –
you would love me, for me.

It's the weight of love,
the shells of depression that crumble into grains of sand;

the same sand that battles Love in a tango for two, that
makes me feel their existence.

Dillon Haas

Ordering In

A jingle of keys hitting the counter sounds,
before the sighs of her frustration(s) –

it's safe to say: work was a cluster-fuck.

As she showers, you prepare a few things;
her favorite food already on its way.

Foot rubs and back scratches in progress,
Netflix whispers in the background as
she opens-up about her day.

You're fired-up with her:
"baby, don't waste your energy on them."

Appreciation dilates within either eye, before she kisses you:
"you know what? – you're absolutely right."

Standing up, you shrug your shoulders as if it's no big deal, before
you steal
a look at how much happier she's become.

But
you can't tell if it's from you, or
from the knocks at the door.

Either way, it's adorable.

Young King

Bells ring as, now, your wall has an opening:

a woman whose hand holds the brick that belongs.

Your lips purse, and your head begins to turn;
you've been here before.

But her eyes grab hold of your face, guiding
your attention to hers, a smile –

a wave of warmth that doesn't come from the sun;
though, one would swear it did.

Together, you begin moving bricks,
so that,
one day,
you can feel the crown that she envisions you wearing.

Without You

It feels as though time has merged into an essence of one;
Daylight losing its meaning as
Nighttime calls my attention like the mockingbird outside my
window –

singing his song of solemnness, car alarms and
other mimicry to pass the time till his other half emerges from the
shadows of solace.

Each sunrise whispering another day closer to the date we will
meet again;
to take the air from within;
to make me feel weightless, once more.

I too hum to his tune,
in the hopes that night will morph to day,
and days to weeks;
until,
eventually,
I'm there humming his song, together, with you.

Soda and Ice

Eating away at cubes of water,

so too, your eyes begin to water –

the way that she looks at you, dissolving something inside of you;

forever wishing they could feel this realization that you have just come to.

Dillon Haas

Sweater Weather

You keep me warm and comfortable;
something most are unable to do.

And,
when you're not with me, I feel naked –
like
something
is
missing

but, that's just the thing –
you're the sweater that keeps me from freezing,
in a world of cruelty and uncertainty.

A person,
such as me,
attempting their best version inside of a reality
of whom no other man could be
towards you in their wildest of dreams.

For someone like you to like me for… me?

Well, then,
you are, indeed, the Queen of any man's dreams.

Blinders

I'm so into you that
I choose
not
to
see
the bad in you,
because we both know the
harm that would do
and potentially misconstrue
the love that I have for you,
solidifying the risk of me losing you.

Lost in the Clouds

The thought of you
has me skipping in the clouds;
though cliché and simple,
it's true.

You,
the gravity that
binds my soul's happiness together –
leaving me looking up at the night sky
with the wish that we will remain forever.

If It's Not Too Much to Ask

She wants to be the
sunlight that caresses your skin,
when you step from the shadows on a cold day.

Or the music, to which,
your body wants to move with.

You

Your smile widens,
those lustful eyes dilating
into something even *you* thought you
didn't possess.

And
you undress
your feelings to show me the real you –
not the old you that *you* created and outgrew,
but,
rather,
the you, that you knew, I could see through.

Mi Amor

There's a chaos in my soul.

Though,
lo and behold,
when I hear your laugh in a crowded room,
I hope you know how much that makes me feel whole.

And, despite the men whose hearts bleed greed,
you will forever remain faithful to me.

Dillon Haas

The Seconds Between Heartbeats

It's your first date with her and
here you are
standing like a confused mad-man;
a wave of thoughts consistently crashing
down in a seductive sea of
imaginative possibilities as to
what she might be wearing.

Others buzz past you –
a swarm of bodies that add to this hive of anxiety that is
your nightmare of heavily populated places.

You rub your knuckles, nervously, as
your heart starts to drum a tune.

*Should I just leave? I wonder if she sees me – is that
her approaching?
No. That's not her. Though, it shouldn't be too hard to find one
another –
she just has to look for the person who looks lost.*

*Or, maybe she's not approaching at all.
Maybe she's watching from afar,
giggling until you walk alone back to your car.*

She said she'd be here, right?

But then your obnoxious brain stops as
there's a tap on your shoulder –
a formidable flood of adrenaline enters your veins as
you slow-motion turn to face her.
And, she's gorgeous – your face tells *her* this.

She blushes, even laughs the cute giggle that you were so worried
about –

though, it wasn't from watching you suffer,
but because she knows, one day, you're going to fall for her.

That's Just It, Isn't It

Work is almost over,
but you haven't been tracking the time;
the way her eyes look at you, replaying in your mind.

The happiness she brings you burns
your cheeks and you can't stop cheesing –
until you finally do.

And that's just it, isn't it –
now you're nervous she'll become just a memory,
a ghost to you.

Dillon Haas

Shoes to Unfill

Your hand squeezes tighter around his,
arms swinging, knuckles white,
your smile whiter.

You're not afraid to show your dimples this time,
nor the deep brown of your eyes –
as sunglasses no longer need to be worn
to mask the marks
that the Ex used to do to you.

This one…
this one seems different.

Double-Dutch

I'm ready to let you in,
to let you see and
fall in love with the *real* me.

But,
then I hesitate;
I remember those who I caught
myself wondering the same thing with, before.

Always the awkward calm before the storm.
The stutter-step towards this being legit.

And now look at me –
only showing you glimpses of who I can be…
who *we* can be.

Cough Drop

You want to speak, but you stop yourself –
the irritation in your throat building.

This isn't your environment, is it.

Your head is spinning.
But, isn't the world *always* spinning?

You're uncomfortable, aren't you.

You grab your throat – it's getting tighter.

But then she makes you laugh, and
you find yourself relaxing around her,
able to speak again.

Rip-Cord

You're letting your guard down for her.
It's frightening; yet, exhilarating, isn't it? –
to feel again.
Do you
pull
the
cord
and float back down to safety?
Or, do you embrace the free-fall to
see where it takes you?

Only time will tell – you're falling, after-all.

Dillon Haas

Sweet Dreams

Before I nod off for the night, I
wanted to say how beautiful and amazing you are as,
not only my woman, but also as a person.

You're consistently there for your friends,
through thick and thin; a reliable shoulder to lean on.
And when they sometimes don't want to hear it,
you tell them anyway. Why?

Well,
it's because you love and know what's best for them –
a friend to the end.

It's those selfless acts that add to the morning sunrises,
which wake me up,
blinding me with the disbelief that
you're in *my* life.

And, like the sun,
you don't realize your self-worth.
So, it's my job to remind you.

Anyways,
I was just thinking about you –
sweet dreams, baby.

| HEARTBREAK |

Dillon Haas

Isn't it Funny

Isn't it funny,

the moments you feel the most connected with the world are
when your heart wants to cry?

You know, that lump you get in your throat? –
the one that wants to drop, but waits for the
tears in either eye to make the first move.

When your chin starts to tremble, and you
whisper aloud "Fuck," because you thought
you could keep it together?

And, suddenly,
you can't escape your bed because all you can muster for the day
is to stare through your ceiling and into the sky
hoping that, when you actually blink, the
feeling will go away? –

while the time you've had together storms
through your brain like a photo album,
until you hear their voice narrate:

"whatever happens in this world,
you are the best thing that's happened to me."

Yeah.

Shards and Shadows

They were your world.

But,
to them, you were just a part of it –

losing pieces of yourself the longer time progressed;

until you were left trying to gather
the shards, atop the silhouette of your former,
that made you,
you.

Purgatory

Trudging through the marsh waters of your memories,
ichor clings at your waist-side – nightmares of
the shit you've been through, adapted to, gave in to.

A lantern lit,
the smell of kerosene clings to your nostrils –
an embrace you could do without, if it wasn't
for the enjoyment of newfound company,
of not feeling so alone in the darkness.

Waist deep, face bleak, sleep
has been eluding you –
a romantic waltz with Insomnia that has left you unrecognizable.

A silver locket amongst the muck is what you're after.
Though, it's not so much the object as it is the initials carved
on the back of it;

letters that you would have recited without hesitation,
but now search for because
you're scared of admitting you've forgotten them
as they have forgotten you.

From Marble

You've watched pieces of yourself shatter to the ground.

To them, you look complete – a God[dess] made from marble.

But they haven't seen all that was taken from you.

A Fool's Garden

At dinner it was all smiles and laughter,
your love for me never to blossom.

We walked to the garden; hands rooted in
fabricated potential.

My back pressed against an oak and
your eyes spidered over me.

You whispered, hesitantly: "*I've – never felt this before,*"
nervous for my response.

Butterflies found my stomach and,
in my head, I thought: "*I'm lucky,*"
but it was never spoken, rather, silenced –
lips and tongue intertwined.

I remember the roses you crushed as your body snaked
closer to mine – lust guising your addiction, your game.

I would come to see you and another man –
another rose for your garden.

You spoke the same words;
though, they were barely heard as
I was left picking up the pieces of my dignity.

The "*I've never felt this before,*" slowly sending butterflies into
another victim,
another prey,
another me.

In that rose garden with the single oak tree,
your beauty came with blood drawing thorns –
and, surely, I was pricked.

A fool for a fool's garden.

I think about those broken roses at your feet.
I wonder whether they were symbolic for history repeating itself.

Broken Promises

Perhaps,
what they say is true:

it's not hard for someone else to find another you.

Though,
you can't help but wonder:
what could have been? –
with the one
whose heart
Love
outgrew.

Dillon Haas

Thundercloud

She never wanted to say it, and neither did I.

The truth too painful; yet, obvious in hindsight.

I knew her first instinct would be to bite her lower lip, nervously.
As she knew I would – to my inner cheek.

Nature's Clock of Gut Feeling, of intuition, had struck
loud and true.
The time for "the conversation" had arrived.

We thought it "fun" to avoid.
And,
at times,
it was.
It made life easier –
to just live and forget that this day would come;
to pretend that things would *always* be fine;
that we were the relationship anomaly.

But, deep down, we both knew it had to happen.

We knew our path that was once one
had finally split – none involving the other.

Her eyes flickered back and forth, begging for
rage and rancor to bubble inside me.
Perhaps, that would have been easier –
to yell, to fight, to hate her.

Though, she found nothing of the sort. And the understanding in
my eyes,
of the acceptance, of the hug that I gave her – letting her know that
the feeling was mutual.
That? –
that was worse than the spectrum.

I don't recall it raining that night,
though water poured down both our faces.

Delusion or Delirium

Confusion blossoms into Disbelief, as
Anger whispers hurtful words to Misery –
your relationship as romantic partners now,
and forever,
a fateful memory.

Nightfall trades shifts with Daylight, but
Tears have welded your eyes shut, so
you've been missing the exchange;
though,
you were never one to sleep, anyway.

In the moments you're able to catch your breath and
stand the sight of yourself in the mirror,
you've debated shutting her out of your life forever.

Yet, upon trembling exhales,
the thought of her ceasing to exist in your mind would
be a nightmare.

Though…
the pain you're enduring now is
something you'd wish to never remember.

Broken Glass

The only brightness these nights come from your iPhone,
when it's 2 AM and you can't sleep;

its energy cupping and framing your face with calloused hands.

Navigating through new notifications, you've grown hopeful –
but, for what reason?

They're with someone else,
happier than you could have made them.

And now,
their hands are around another –
while the only embrace you have is
from a shattered screen and a shattered self-esteem.

Dillon Haas

Reflection Pond

It's easy to hate yourself, when
the pain he's caused

sends shockwaves across your soul.

Like that of ripples in a pond, he distorts your image.

It's only when he's out of your life, that
you can truly appreciate your own reflection.

Dillon Haas

Pushing Away

If you could be free of the memory of me,

would you?

A Bird Without a Cage

Tree limbs yawn,
stretching their wisdom into the air without a care.

Swaying in the breeze,
your feathers rustle, but
it's not from the wind.

Rather,
the thought of someone close wanting to see your wings clipped;

to control you;

to take away what it *truly* means to be free.

Dillon Haas

Cold Sweats

Here you are,
under the covers,
a few drinks recovered and
your mind begins to stumble
down
the
steps
of
your
memories;
cursed with the trouble(s)
of losing the one who made
your heart thunder
like the rain clouds above you,
puddling desolation down your face.

Dillon Haas

Slavery of the Soul

You're starving yourself of the person you are meant to be,

confined in the chains of another's misery.

Better to walk alone,

than with that of false company.

Dillon Haas

Backspace (sister piece)

They might not notice it now but, when you remove yourself from
their life,
the realization of them taking you for granted will
flood their innermost thoughts.

It won't happen immediately, but panic will begin to set in;
their daily routine seemingly off as you are no longer a part of it –
the faces they force never matching the missing puzzle piece
that *is* you.

Familiar adventures, smells,
even the simple cadence and lingo of another will
drive them out of the present and into nostalgia.

For them,
they will forever feel the fearful realization of
you being the one that got away.

Call Me Crazy (sister piece)

Isn't it wild how you can love someone so much

that they become a part of you?

Your jokes,
even your lingo, mirror their own.

And, now that they're gone,
your body knows a piece of you has been cut out,

so it tries to heal itself with
Nights of silent tears,

because salt supposedly heals all wounds?

Call me crazy.

Dillon Haas

Restless Nights

I think I stay up late because, I know,

a new day means another night without you.

New Days to Come

It's interesting to be at peace, during
the darkest moments of Love's release.

To understand self-reliance and
the importance in staying true to one's own,
Emerson would, surely, be proud.

Your chin remaining high, **you** fix your crown –
for, Nature can be brutal and Life, at times, cruel.

But Love can be shattering –

may she be a lesson, for the kindness you have
roaring inside of you.

Metamorphosis

Sleep has lost its name, as
each night feels as though you have an exam you
didn't prepare for the following morning.

While dread has replaced adrenaline –
For, Their face no longer brings you joy,
but sadness.

Weightless

With the air Spartan-kicked from your chest,

you're free-falling into a tunnel of blackness,
while your hands reach out in front of you for
them to choose you.

But, in all honesty, you don't know if they will –

they could just lean over and watch as
you plummet into oblivion.

Dillon Haas

Night and Day

Familiar footfalls and laughter clatter amongst the walls
you've built.

An eerie sound, as Night tolls her bell –
signaling for the noise of Day to come to an end.

Your face illuminates from a closely clutched candle –
two wicks drowned in flame,
each dancing closer, but never touching;

its warmth feels kind.
Though, Night's subtle chills still slither down your spine,
hissing and urging for you in wasting no more time.

And, so, you begin to walk along, together –
one hand clutched with hers, the other your source of warmth.

She brings you to the laughter:
Shadowy Ruins of
a ghost-town kingdom you've built –

memories vaulted away,
forged from a time of better and brighter days.

But you've been avoiding them.

For, it's easier to forget during the noise of Daylight's hours,
than to sit with Night and relive
memories that led to them breaking your heart.

Ripples

Words that you say to her don't go unnoticed –

they ripple back to a vault of memories in the subconscious
like waves kissing an ocean's shore,
salt meeting sand,
only to reappear in her night-time thoughts when she can't sleep,
nor stand the idea of you.

And you think words carry no meaning.

Dillon Haas

Sleep Tight

You're up in your thoughts – the 3 AM type of late and
you hear his phone D I N G.

After a few more silent breaths, it starts to make your head ring –
the glow from across the room reminds you you're
not the only one who can't sleep.

But,
you try to,
despite the Devil opposite of you.

Your heart's racing, even though you whisper for it not to.

Now the sun is seeping through the blinds as
your "man" rolls over – his love for you blind.

Burly arms envelope around you,
the weight of his snores letting you know "He's got you."

Though, you know it's not true,
and
it's not just you.

Dillon Haas

An Ode: To Those Who Self-Destruct

You've been hurt and fucked over so many times, in the past, that
you're waiting for this one to do the same.

Rather than enjoying the love that they've
shown you already,
your mind spirals into infamous and self-destructive "what ifs."

Questions are meant to come off as figurative,
but conversations soon turn argumentative.

And, now, your insecurity is extremely unattractive.

*

We get it –
you wanted to bring that person closer…but,
you only ended-up pushing them further and further away.

Until, eventually,
their touch just became another memory.

Dillon Haas

Forever is Funny

This cigarette
smoke,
which scratches
the back of
my throat,
still
isn't
as
toxic
as
you.

Rainy Day Fund

You're tired of being taken for granted, and
now you can't stand him –
his spell over you is fading, perhaps even disenchanted?

You're looking for that Folgers Coffee container labeled:
"Chances Left to Give Him."

You look left, then right, before
nearly tearing off the top to what remains for you to give.

Yet, now you find yourself unable to open the lid –
this time, it's different;
the weight of his presence on your skin feels lighter.

You're left with the nail-biter thought of:
What now?

Now, he gets no more chances.

Now, you can run off to do what makes *you* feel liberated and free
from that toxic excuse of a man and
live the life that *you've* always planned.

Dillon Haas

Cooking Up & Splitting Up

It's funny,
he's eating the meal that he expected you to cook for him. Yet,
as you look down at yours and begin eating,
this time,
yours feels a little colder.

Body Count

Who even are you?

Take a look at you –
she took the skin off her back,
showed the heart on her sleeve,
for you.

How is it
you can be ready to leave, so soon?

Take a look at you –
feeling nothing when
sadness and confusion river down her face.

And, the craziest thing is
you're ready to do it all again with another.

Who even are you?

Dillon Haas

My Book Collection

I was young.

I remember hiding my favorite book, so
that no one else could feel how it made me feel.

I was young.

I remember losing him –
not because I didn't want him to see the world
but,
because,
I didn't want the world to share him with me;
to have them feel how he made me feel.

I was young.

Wishbone

I'm staring at your shadow,
or,
rather,
what would have been your seat at Thanksgiving Dinner.

But,
you made the choice to make me look like an idiot.

And, now, here I am –
looking like the fool
who fell for the man
that played me.

The same girl who holds
the wishbone –
whose wish is
to see your stupid face, one more time.

Dillon Haas

Snakes in Your DM's

Broken words and dissonant whispers
don't hit as hard as that
late night notification:
"you up?"

Of course, you are,
but not because of the reason(s) he wants.

You leave him on *read*, amongst the others.

Dillon Haas

Light Switch

His smile turns you on,
but his actions turn you off.

His whispers raise goosebumps,
but the cops at your door
let you know that you won't be going to sleep anytime soon.

Don't worry babe, I'll change.

You laugh,
knowing damn well the only thing that needs to change
is your mindset and love for him.

He's a light switch that can't stay on or off,
and you're just the energy that he doesn't mind wasting.

Slow-Mo

I think about the time when your eyes searched for
forgiveness in mine,

holding my attention hostage as you
whispered the words:
I cheated.

It was then –
you saw the reflection of your world ending,
before the sound of my heart's detonation.

In What World Were You Mine

A moment in time that will forever change you,
is when their daily texts stop coming –

the love in their heart, for you,
no longer humming. And

you're left holding your phone, awaiting their notification.
But it will never happen.

It is then, you'll be at your lowest –

sitting with the lights off. Though, the TV
in your place is still playing, so that the voices onscreen
mask the silence of you feeling so alone. And
you can't help but wonder:

despite it all,
how is it possible for two kindred souls to grow so far apart when,
during the time of your relationship,
you were so fucking close….

Like, at one point, you both envisioned growing old together.

But now you're left to contemplate:

in what world's timeline did you two remain together?

Dillon Haas

Neophobia

The thought of starting afresh
makes you nervous –

retelling your story to a new lover,
reintroducing another to your family,
the list goes on.

You don't stay with the toxicity because you
hope they'll change.

You stay with the toxicity, because they're predictable;

they're easier to manage than starting over.

Or so,
you lie to yourself.

Dillon Haas

Venom

Why is it,
when you remove someone from your life,

they try to slither back in?

Almost as if
their soul uncoiled from within, awakening
to the scent of your self-love;

their forked tongue never admitting their wrongings.

And now they think they can break-in
and erase the damage they've already tattooed upon your skin,

by sinking their fangs into the memories you've had together,
hoping to paralyze you;
to entrap you,
forever.

Dillon Haas

Broken-Up

It just feels like we aren't even best friends anymore.

I'm not sure if it's because you want to heal without me there,
or if it's because you really don't think about me anymore.

And I'm not trying to make you mad, sad, or invoke a reaction by
writing this. But I think if we were to be *just* friends, shouldn't we
at least act as we were? –

unless, what you want is for me to be gone.

I just… don't know what to do in this dilemma.

Because, if we continue to be distant, I'll feel that our
friendship is forever fading, too.

The Distance Between Us

Hands were held just a moment ago.

But now you've stormed off, because
you had to make a point –

showing him that he can't just say things like that to you;
that words sting just as much as physical blows.

But having a conversation about it wouldn't
give you the same sense of satisfaction
as that face he wears far behind you –

dumbfounded as to what it was he said
to create such a distance between the two of you;
metaphorically, and quite literally.

Chapstick

Filling the cracks and mending their pain.

You wet their lips,
just for them to whisper another's name.

A pawn to their game;

to be used and
forgotten,

until
they end up replacing you.

Dillon Haas

| MENTAL HEALTH |

Dillon Haas

Smoke Stories

I was so high one time
that my best friend said it was because

the weed was smoothing out my brain's wrinkles.

And, till this day,
that's the funniest fucking description I've ever heard.

2:30 AM

Lost in your own head,
a lighter and joint in hand.

Time seems to slow,
your playlists also in rotation;

Life reflecting its meaning amongst the night-time stars.

Moments, such as this, made you closer to yourself,
to the world;

weeding out those who wavered your flame.

With a long exhale,
head slowly bobbing,
feet tapping,
body vibing,

you realize Art is the reason for your existence –
to endure pain, in order to create for others.

Body High

A single flame cuts through the darkness,
igniting magic to which you inhale.

Breathing out,
your world goes upside down;
yet, right-side up as,

now,

you're seeing things in a more loving way.

Finding Yourself

I'm sure the traumas,
or the insecurities of others, have
physically and figuratively beaten down who you were as a child,
as a person.

The beautiful complexity of your mind was made to
feel anything but.
And so, as a result, your personality changed.

Perhaps this is the reason so many people admit to
the shift of happiness they once had,
from the time of when they were younger,
to now.

But look at the growth of you –
surviving your own battles,
your own struggles.

Scars that prove you're mortal;
yet, your newfound self-love is something otherworldly.

I'll Have Another

When you were little,
you told your batting coach that you would
never become like your mother –

a tempest who prioritized drinking and swearing to
temporarily forget the other half, that was no longer a part of her.

But slowly you become older and
find drinks in your hand; each one a little colder
than the last.

And that's when you wonder –
are you becoming her?

Lifeline

You're disoriented under the darkness of ocean waves,
your lungs feeling the weight within the breath that's held –

a poetic injustice to the pain you've felt of the past as
those same ocean waves crest above you,
looking down in memorial.

If this was a Kate Chopin novel,
you'd be doing yourself a service.

But it's not –
it's real life and
you dig your feet into the sand that was almost called home,

pushing with the last of your energy, your hope,

rocketing upward to the light of what
could only be the sun
so that you can,
once again,
find solace.

Dillon Haas

Woe is Me

you've changed.

things don't seem as bright as they once did
when you were younger –
a time when you were ignorant to the painful truths of the world.

now, as you grow older,
Forlornment fills your mind and
embraces the warmth of Misery.

vines of new emotion begin their constriction around all
that is touched by Joy, as
Darkness trades stories with Abandonment in
a tavern that *is* your inner thoughts.

Panic and her counterpart, Anxiety, grab a drink next to them,
waving you over to join –
do you join?
or, do you squeeze your eyes and say
that the world isn't capable of malevolence.

you've made your decision, a decision that the younger you
wouldn't have otherwise done, and
you walk towards your demons.

their presence draws a welcoming warmth, long overdue.
their brutal honesty is what makes you feel alive,
in the moment.

suddenly, everything doesn't seem so dark as
it once did before.

perhaps that's what Nature intended –
to make friends with what lies in the dark,
to face your fears,
your demons.

Depression and Friends are forbidden fruits that
wish to be loved,
as you once loved your Imaginary Friends, long ago.

Sleep Demon

Your mind and body have abandoned you,
trapped inside a dream.

Eyes wide,
hallucinations alive:
demons and shadows of the room meld into
one of the same.

Frozen in place,
limbs unresponsive,
realization hits: escaping the present is
no longer an option.

Fear closing in,
you feel: the weight of your breaths,
a cry to move,
beads of sweat that allude to
the danger born anew.

Sleep Paralysis hovering over you,
eyes locked –
your heartbeat the only sound screaming for it all to stop.

Schizophrenia

Years of pain wash away with the laughter of another –
their energy tracing the source of trauma that is
your damaged past.

Talking about stories most people wouldn't get,
but *they* do.

Conversations are effortless.
Conversations become *interesting*.

Suddenly,
you can actually live in the present –
shit just clicking
without the worry of what to say next,
because they got you.

Out of body,
you're left to look down at an actual genuine moment –

a stranger to your own skin.

Prison of the Mind

Stumbling down
a tunnel, deep within catacombs,
cold and wet cobblestone caress your calloused skin,
reminding you you're not alone.

The pitter-patter as you walk along;
feet bare, eyes glazed over. A conversation of
footsteps and whispers; an exotic harmonization.

Creepy, true – but, you pretend to stay strong.

You reach a cell: walls of bone, brick and stone;
layers, in which, feed to your insomnia – from night,
till morning dawn.

Below you, scribbled on the floor, words once written in shadow
cling to your conscious –
as if an ornamental on a tree that's lost its leaves,
lost its color.

You don't turn, but
you hear

the exit close as you've been buried alive; lost and smothered.

Depression: A Modernist's Approach

You find yourself collecting amongst particles of dust –
unmoving; yet, strangely, existing.

Bedroom curtains closed,
you still feel the grayness of the sky outside.

When will the weather pass? You don't know.

And so,
you continue to lay
motionless
in
time,
while time consumes you.

Simple, Yet Complex, as a Weed

You're persistent –

sprouting through the cracks of society;
wiggling your way to the sunlight, because
you prefer to stay out of the under-dark.

When you're free, above the ground, away from those
dragging you down, it's
then that people begin to notice you; grow disdain for you.

They notice you because, when they step on you,
you don't let that kill you.

You're a survivor.

You're a warrior who won't accept defeat,
until defeat is the only option.

But, that's the thing.

You always come back.
You always resurrect stronger than before.

Untitled

There's a journey of events that one goes through;
wishing that some portion of their plan would come true.

Though,
for one to enter into
a version of this person's self, seems too
far and in-between to relate to.

Because we're all walking down our own avenue,
taking in the simplicities of nature – such as morning mildew,
to pay attention to a version of ourselves that we outgrew.

Superstition

The reason that rubber-band around your wrist goes from

fitted to expanded, during the week, is not really

from the bad energy it absorbs from your body;

like a Dream Catcher of sorts.

Though, it's fun to pretend –

to throw out that stretched band,

slip a smaller new-one on and

go about your week with "guaranteed" good vibes.

Monsters from Men

Black boots and even blacker souls march with evil tattooed.

Nose to the floorboards, dirt rains down upon you,
your back pinned to the ground –

though, it's not unlike them to see you at your lowest.

Hair slicked-back, cigarettes become lit.
The smell of their smoke hits different than from the camp your
father went to.

While your eyes peak through the crevices,
not unlike the bars that contained your mother and brothers.

To be suppressed in fear;

To be made to *feel* beneath them;

To witness what separates the Monsters from the Men.

Dillon Haas

Loose Leaf

Never bound; yet, promised belonging.

The lines upon your surface await
to tell their story, and

it's your fear that you'll remain wordless;
to be ignored, or worse – discarded.

Dillon Haas

Like the Moon

It's sort of crazy –
you've created a world of fantasy for people to escape to;
yet, they escape that too.

You know it's not because of your talent for writing –
because that shit is fuel for fumes.

And
if they didn't give up so soon
they would realize,
like the moon,
it contains phases:
chapters that morph till the masterpiece is shown.

Shackles that Don't Cling

Calloused from the air you breathe.

Day to day slurs – a toxic cloud to which you wish to be freed.

A nation of Freedom but, in which, Racism bleeds.

How easy a life can be taken… and from just one knee.

Dillon Haas

Dementia

Free falling: arms embracive, mind erasing.

Memories, like photographs, rain down around you.

Evasive and out of reach, you still attempt to
collect your favorite ones –

because, in the end,
no one wishes to be alone in their own head.

Mousetrap

Your mind has hit a wall.
But where do you begin?

The steps toward your future just on the other side,
though feeling so out of reach –
like a mousetrap, you're tempted to
risk the worst, in order to
achieve greatness.

The sight too good to be true,
you can't help but to feel so small
in a world of constant competition and corruption.

So, you plot.

You weigh out your decisions because,
unlike the rest,
you will not fall.

The Sheep Who Thinks He's the Wolf

There are sheep out there in wolves clothing –
sheep, because they're not strong enough to make a woman happy;
yet, they put on the façade that they have something to offer.

Perhaps, they do:
instability, immaturity, and a lack of intellect.

The same ones who make posts bashing women;
who prowl on insecurity.

The ones who complain "there are no good ones left;"
who feel entitled they're *owed* something.

To the Sheep who thinks he's the Wolf –
may you not get caught by the real pack.

Method to the Muscle

Weights became your therapy, your meditation;
it refrained you from doing something stupid in a
world that is notoriously unforgiving and unpredictable;
yet, rewarding and beautiful.

In those moments of metal clanking solitude,
it left you to work on yourself – a tune that you grew to
love; to recognize as each rep built a new part of you,
a stronger you,
a wiser you.

Your body reacted extremely well to this self-infliction of
building and breaking muscle fibers, and
a new addiction began to grow –
you were *really* good at something.

People left you alone.
People admired you.
People began to *notice* you.

Though, as you grew older, you realized that
the one true super-power is that of which people
cannot see, unless they grow close –
your mind and your wit.

The nervous tissue that craves to be worked-on,
craves to be challenged.

The muscle that isn't a muscle – yet, seems to grow stronger as
one would.

New Year, New Growth

Be the you that the younger you thought would
never be a possibility – to branch away from
a world full of constant judgement and
negativity. Build your team with both
old friends, and new –
be strong, be
brave;
do
not
be
afraid
to cast
aside
those who
are weak,
and to keep
those who
want
to
blossom
like
you.

This is Growing Up

Childhood memories are fallen sycamore leaves.

You're running around outside
gathering them up,
before it's too late.

But,
would you look at that –
they're finally gone with the wind that
is your busy work schedule.

People rarely reminisce anymore.

Social Media

You're terrified about what
others might think, so
you've been shelving everything internally and
sadistically smiling in the mirror at
whoever this "you,"
that *you* created,
is.

Little do you know,
people will notice this persona and
will open
its closet doors labeled: Insecurities,

grabbing one leg out, after the next,
until the skeletons of your closet
are brushing off their dust and smiling
back at you in that very same mirror.

By now, your smile has faded, and you're nervous –
your secret is out.

What?! You've never contemplated the possibility? Ha ha.

Oh, don't get me started on your friends – mind you,
you've been surrounding yourself with those who
are doing the same –
lashing out and consistently comparing oneself for
some toxic, fabricated, personal gain.

Dillon Haas

Fiction Becomes Reality

You feel a metallic barrel of a 45 enter your mouth, and
the trigger is pulled.

Sitting there,
a taste of a hundred copper pennies are fresh upon your tongue,
a
little
hint
of
brain-matter, and
a giant hole in the back of your head –
of which welcomes a subtle sea-breeze.

For a moment, it's actually sort of nice –
the void of nothingness, and the sand washing over your feet.

Meanwhile, Writer's Block wastes no time and cleans off her gun.

Dillon Haas

Tricked: A Concrete Jungle

Are we truly free in the hours of the day?

Most of which are pertained
to activities that numb us from our inner-most thoughts and
pay us by the hour –
slapped with the disguised name of 'career,' or 'job.'

Whilst the remaining hours of the night
are credited to downing a fifth of
Tito's Vodka to
temporarily silence the demons in your head.

But, wait, there's more.

The best part is you wake back up into this nightmare
and you slowly forget the things that
once made you happy because,
NEWSFLASH,
your homeowner is increasing rent and
you better go make more money.

It's terrifying, truly.

We've become so enveloped in this system of commerce
and success,
imprisoned behind psychological barriers and prescription
medications that
we think it's normal.

Instead, we've become tricked –
tricked to stay deep inside this jungle made of concrete.

Connect with me:

Instagram: d.m.haas
Website: Dillonhaasbooks.com